A STRAIGHT UP GIANT

Mark Waldron was born in New York in 1960 and grew up in London. He lives in East London with his wife and son, and began writing poetry in his early 40s. He published two collections with Salt, *The Brand New Dark* (2008) and *The Itchy Sea* (2011), which were followed by three from Bloodaxe, *Meanwhile, Trees* (2016), *Sweet, like Rinky-Dink* (2019) and *A Straight Up Giant* (2023).

MARK WALDRON

A Straight Up Giant

BLOODAXE BOOKS

ISBN: 978 1 78037 669 1

First published 2023 by
Bloodaxe Books Ltd,
Eastburn,
South Park,
Hexham,
Northumberland NE46 1BS

www.bloodaxebooks.com
For further information about Bloodaxe titles
please visit our website and join our mailing list
or write to the above address for a catalogue.

Supported using public funding by
ARTS COUNCIL
ENGLAND

Cover design: Neil Astley & Pamela Robertson-Pearce.

Printed in Great Britain by Bell & Bain Limited, Glasgow, Scotland, on
acid-free paper sourced from mills with FSC chain of custody certification.

ACKNOWLEDGEMENTS

Some of these poems have appeared in *The Poetry Review*, *Anthropocene* and *Poetry London*. 'In the wayward place' was commissioned by Rachel Whiteread for a show at Gagosian. I want to thank Edwina Attlee, Wayne Holloway-Smith, Matthew Dickman, Ahren Warner, Martha Sprackland, Ben Rogers and Julie Hill for their advice on the manuscript.

CONTENTS

I am not a bad bird

Why do we love you, world, when you run away from us?
You keep running away, and yet we still love you.

ALCUIN OF YORK

Panic Room

so here we are then
safely in the safe space

in with the alligator toothpaste

and the hermetic plumbing

in with the inside
and its lumpy specificities

its spongy chandeliers
which bedeck the envelope

its charming armadillo
cutting a rug

rub this rub-a-dub plush between your pinkies

taste the boisterous canapés

there's adequate room for two
if you'll only slide along a bit

besides
where else is there for us to go
now the sun's coming up

and out on the outside
in the placard fields
and the serried woods

the furious leaves are harvesting
the day's first light

chugging down the brand new light

Hippopotami at the Water Hotel

There were four secret turtle teeth

hidden inside the water hotel bedside table drawer

My hush-hush aide-de-camp (hippopotamus disguise
crab-like sideways gait)

had sploshed through our room
and snuck them in there
while we were downstairs snorkelling

for Vietnamese seaweed and chatterbox whelks

Her purpose in so doing was
and still is
something of a tough nut to crack

I loved her to pieces despite the fact
she was unpredictable
classificd and possibly a little unglued

It's funny how you can fervently want someone
even when they're completely
clandestine and about as clear as dishwater

(Perhaps it's just the other's scent we love
The rest –
the look of them
the way they move
their cleverness and kindliness being only bottling)

Her tough skin surface brought to mind a scuffed old suitcase
which had been lugged up and down rattling gangplanks
as it toured the Persian Gulf in the 1920s
in the possession of a Belgian lady of a certain age
thin as a rake
specs
upset stomach
flat shoes

I never saw my aide out of her potamus cozzie

or
come to that

myself out of mine

The orange winter sun paused just above the horizon of Clapton, mid-rise flats. It gave off no discernible heat, and seemed just a picture of itself, but the light was still blinding, so that one was forced to look away.

Swapping Clothes with a Friend

He'd waited till they had cooled

and the sullen ghost of scent
had risen partially off them

and then he'd put them on

had crouched to tie
the someone else's laces

stood and zipped himself inside their pants

buttoned up his body
in their shirt

each button intimately privy to his touch

before he'd then looked down

      upon this brand new surrogate in all its
      fine-grained paucity

and here the other comes in a straight line swerve

he sees the shoes he had been wearing

      ushered down into the patterns of the parlour carpet

he sees the stammered natter of his clothes

his watch that inches shyly on their wrist
       his par-baked smile

his hands held out admitting helplessness or loss

the armchairs stiff in bully suits
the papered walls

the caged bird bites her bars

what have we done with ourselves

come over this way and sit with me you old minotaur

      it's ok to be afraid

How a Poem Works

knocking on

they purloin an inflection such as I don't know

then they slide it over   picking up some of what it slides over

        it's sticky I should have said

and surfaces are a given what with the whole ball of wax
and the specifics which excite

colour is splurged all over in a headlong reference to place

do you remember when we hid in the Pantone® 5605
as though there was no today

and the ground
was all present and correct and enacting a roisterous context

there ought to be a barely detectable best foot forward
as well as a nod to the prevailing climate

        cog teeth speak flap tongued of the method

and dots
and an ending that lets you down so you can step off it effortlessly

back into your day your articulated day without breaking your stride

changed but entirely unchanged

(Implacable doom-trod sky notwithstanding

happy fire might caper through
the dry rooms of the heart

might run barefoot chortle chortle lick lick chortle

for the past is ice cream

      no wait
      is a picture of ice cream

      it just might blister up wonderfully

and the whole placid house

           thinking it pretty

                for a time sit still for it lick chortle

well burn the baby fire right off

      give it back burned

such illegal caverns to spy in a fire's royal tummy)

There was a time I wanted to tell you everything. Or perhaps I should say there was a time I wanted to tell you at least something, something from which you might glean or build some kind of everything.

A Feather in My Cap

A Tuesday, and the chimney welled out its billows
which blundered up
rollicking over and over into a baby sky.

I kept the Ningbing false antechinus lodged in my barchetta pocket
so close to my ear that I could hear her raspy breath as she chewed
a bit of bluish-green raffle ticket, which,

once upon a time, had won a small piece of absolutely nothing
as a take-home from a school fête.

For the most part I adopted the upward dog as a diversion,
while twin violins
powder-puffed the whole locale with stop-start bait and switch.

Out on the border of their audibility, down beyond the railings
of the great arboretum, birds tensed and withdrew,

withheld that which
they had been on the point of laying.

Snatches of the Takemitsu wandered into my regard
like austere cattle –
waxed and frightened, glimpsed through shifting maiden silvergrass.

My pocket was a coffin. The tiny marsupial's immersion in it

a dreamfood
a straight up giant
a dreamfood

I meant to have you leave the premises with a party bag inside which would be a rubber giraffe perhaps, one with a wire frame embedded in it (so that it might be coerced into all manner of different positions), and a little seam running round it, which would speak in a quiet unassuming voice, of the mould it had emerged from, just as our navels refer back to our own moulds. Would you return, or so the argument went, if I hadn't presented you with at least a small token, a thing which would at once both describe and ameliorate, possibly even diminish some of this distance between us?

Tender is the born

press on

for I have copied in
the tortoise

the driven tortoise

by which I mean piloted

by which I mean
fire and forget

he goes about thither and there
proud of his niche niche

shell-happy

(would we have chosen a carapace

or are our shells the clevers
we creep inside
when we are hungered for)

come up off the page hammy old son
tortoise friend

rise up off it

      and look at a world
which won't fit
into itself

we cannot ever get it
back in

so what shall we call
     our runaway tale

     tender is the born
     it is the season for it
     a chequered daffodil
     you choose
tortoi
     you choose

A Trap or a Net

birds go on a bony ground

plastic novelties – yay big –

are held in place by a twill weave

while a hard breeze carries our scent off
and occasions the entire apparatus

to bob and twitch with the great mother's
spasmodic rhythm

there's a simple music

it's the distant sound of what must be

      an ice cream van
dolled down
in the small town

where a red-faced boy reaches up

            with a thick coin

so now we wait a short while

the wind will soon be blown away

the trap is nicely laid
        its prey already yours

Perhaps I hoped to take, in return for that modest receptacle with its interred curio, something from you. The look of you clutching it in front of your stomach, perhaps that would be reward enough – the expression of uncertain gratitude parked on your face like a small, pale blue Nissan, as you held your present, as yet unbagged. So like a child you seem standing there; and yet also, so not.

eleven grim poems

Blossom

Once there lived a brother and sister

twins called Blossom and Blossom

Blossom was cruel and kind

In the forest I say they dwelt
and were as poor

as a humperdink moon dipped in nothing worth saying
and lost down the back of a cosmos

Blossom was smarter than a mouse in a homemade
catskin jumpsuit

(bowtie of cat liver whisker-stitched)

Blossom was quiet and loud
and silly and smart

Both were species afar from the lumbering tree
who lugs his preposterous weight

and who is witness to all the quick quick slow

Blossom and Blossom got bitten off face down
by wolves running on foreign law

        A witch awoke

breaks brittle sticks quick for the oven

Something good leaks out of the world
Something bad leaks in

The Garrulous Horse

Once on a time

I went out for a crawl
in calamitous sunshine

and a horse across the road said to me

What are you looking at

The young cobbler who is me crawled on
as if the horse had not spake

I see a femininity in you continued the nag
That womanliness which manifests in the faces of men on their deathbeds

as if a cosy girl rose up from within them
to occupy the space where a man's countenance had once rightfully reigned

When the glamorous young prince (still me)
repaired to his castle (house)

he said to his chambermaid (wife) *My pillow is so old and thin*

I should throw him out but I cannot because I'm in love with him

Is he a bit like me asked the bosomy maid

No he's a bit like me said the miserable old king

     and they lived happy together
                   for all their lives

The Bitten Ball

A little gold princess (solid)

Oh dear butter and shine and cost

played with her ball in the palace garden
every diddle day long

She cherished it
She favoured it beyond her stick and hoop

beyond her wooden dolls

and her automaton which clacked across
the plastic lawns

crying salted tears
which spilled from a lackey-filled reservoir

Then one day that ball was tricked by
a gust of wicky wind

and fell down yonder toytown water well

Deep was the well
and lost
was the ball

(how blankly gone objects linger
How they look up as if to say *what of it?*)

Wot oft?

Wot oft, wot oft? the ball is lost! sang chiffchaff

That frog down there

also gold but bumpy as a toad

he bit upon the spangly ball with stiffened lips
snipped it to let the magic wink come out

I shall have the wink for me he intoned
in a disgusting voice

Damn the spoiled princess

How the godless golden frog widened wide his smile
and then widened it still wider

till he split in two

and all the wink that he had pinched fell out
and sloshed

about the bottom of the well where it slosheth still

A Goodly Fly

Once on a moment

there dwelt a princely fly

(I loved his colour so secret and so on show)
(his jaunty worn prince's headpiece)

(his shameful buzz)

What a fly say I

In those years when the earth was long and doltish

flies tarried
dotting the homescape willingly

and what are you for
soft and loose with your dug gumption holed in your bones

The fly was soon to be married to a ravenous bird

Shh

Live happily

gone off

morrow lemony pom

an orchard

nobod there
except an under the table mediaevalist beloitering in
　　　particoloured cotehardie

and his wimpled mistress

re-enactment parts just like ours

canters left to right
　　　　　　　a liveried manticore chic as nougat

is that you befrolicking off in the betown besquare

　　　snood
　　　early knickers
　　　smile like cheesecake like a bottom bared

rudimentary plosives

pip pip

pip pip
BANG

apple everywhere
everything everywhere

The Traumatised Fox

Once time a fox screams so thick
he blows his pants clean off

those pants (tail on) land on the lake
splish
(troubling the surface only somewhat)

what the fox had witnessed –

deep in forest
where men and laws get well
and properly lost
a bad house had demolished its occupants
a man a woman and the special
child they had named ash

first it broke their bones in slamming doors
then it pressed them hard and hard again
betwixt its walls

then it ran its mangle banisters across their meat
then it sieved their juices through its rugs

and all the while the house bricks crunched against
their mortar

and windows flexed with a tremulous moan
like the sound
of an old fellow's pleasure at a young woman's touch

o now a thin wind
blows in as a nasty nighty night

still the fox's pants
float out on the lickety lake

and through its open door
the wicked house it burps an greasy reek of carnivore

bottomless fox shivers

what is right goes out like a

like a light

How horrid sometimes seemed the adults. And how lost to all of us down here with our sweet privacies. I have still, the small boy I once was. I keep him in the omphalos, and from there he pilots the blundering frame; the lurching, rattling assemblage which must perform the crummy work of grownuphood.

The Woodman Prince

in a kingdom
lit by lashings of sunshine and due process

there once lived a handsomely assembled woodman who would turn

      just like that

into a nicely put together prince and then back

into the woodman

and then again into the prince and then the woodman

                     and then the prince

and then the woodman and then the prince

the changes occurred with an arbitrary frequency

sometimes they burst rapid as the splutters of a guttering candle

or the flickers of an ailing bulb

and other times he would settle for a while into one or other of the states
and would look around tentative

increasing in confidence that he might have solidified once and for all

around the axle of
        whatever that manifestation happened to be

only to suddenly judder for a moment with the sound
of the grinding of gears

before his appearance switched back
                              to that of the rustic woodman

with an unkempt beard or to that

          of the suave and clean-shaven prince
with a jewelled ballock knife tucked into his belt

o but how the maidens were mad for him in each

               of his modes   and kissed him

in reiterant and headlong kisses so that they and their friends
might shriek when he switched
                              mid-kiss

and then the young women would all jump up and down
            and clap with happiness and fright and the woodman

                   or the prince would laugh along with them every
time the switcheroo came upon him in their presence

what stripe of misdeed had the old tailor committed

that a curse that dumb should have stitched his innocent son

Fungi

time a upon once

      when mush spake fruity

and bird blushed torrid neath feathery veneer

a tableau was –

jagged yet not unapproachable peaks
      partake of the distance

the material atop disposed in the manner of a turreted castle

one or two clouds ensure the sky need not be entirely blue

a wishy daytime moon sulks
up in her long coventry of orbit

forest glade

      bush
tiny-flower-platted

a comely king bobs across on a cockhorse

lording it chivalric

saddled up balls and all

heraldic nibnabs

somewhat uncomfy in armour

and the scampering girls and boys
who have not as yet
grown such pungent odours

as trail from kings and queens and commoners
in wispy banners advertising magic

and the whole scenarioriorio

      with its from here to there

gets off scot free

talky shrooms and king and all

        thick with hidden hair

The Piece of String

deeply
        down in wooden woods

      the sleepy children rub their eyes

while groundling beasts snuffle dirt
        for what they might find in it

birdsong palavers the bushes

and over here
a string is tied to a tree

while its other end leads into a hole in the floor

only to emerge once more
as it creeps from a second hole

some six leagues distant in a field of olden cow

illuminated

      they fly their bubbled moos like kites
on the yellow sky

there's the quiet scent of paper

        and barn door words as tall as things

tug this end of the string
      fair cow
          for the spell to break

            and the pop-up world to fold back down
              to sleepydom

Little Men

What is an uptown man but a blurt

                                        chinny chin chin

        but a plea   chinny chin chin

        tenderised by this rickety peace he's living in

                This peace that hangs as poison fruit in the tree tree trees

Three little men

dot dot dot

I'll blow your top in
I'll rasher you streaky
I'll bite your little house right off   with my to-attention teeth

                        Rows of soldiers

hid for now   behind   the plump hedges of their come-hithers

                What type of king is making the roof go in little men

What kind of king

Chinny chin chin

           Let me in

The Princess and the Pea

In the castle's royal chambers

dim lanterns
cast stiff shadows of full-armoured guards

    across the granite floors

        – flicked their breastplates ring and tickle –

        – their furious butch faces hid neath visored helms –

In an alcove
a tapestry rhubarbs

    On a rug
    a wolfhound breaks perspicacious wind

Now look perchance

at wot lies under

fiddling the pastries

    knocking the books

spinning the pulse

Because whatever it is down there   it's mine

I have sometimes wondered if, inside that party bag, I ought to place some kind of apparatus, a gadget of some description which, with the simplest of instructions, you could employ to make, or find, or hunt, or catch, your own small trinket. It would be a device which might harvest nicknacks from the atmosphere of your own dominion, as certain voluminous nets are utilised hereabouts in the gathering of butterflies.

Is it Honey

over here over there wee wee wee

or is it just some kind of look-see   a sing-along

          it *is* honey

or is it just some sort of conduct which might enhance one piglet old chum

you could welly up the atmosphere
               over here over there wee wee wee
when rabbit happens   cross comma fuzzy   declares it isn't honey

bother

it *is* honey

this little piggy trots proximate   this little piggy go home
          nose p-p-pink with excitement

over here over there wee wee wee

piglet obtains that the honey is of a sunny disposition

               his toes in their itness are each

it *is* honey

pooh ray pooh we are in here somewhere   belly up

      making off meat out of loss tiddely pom

over here over there wee wee wee

it *is* honey

Burn Down

The trees rise up burn down

the trees rise up
and burn down

Dear reader
I don't even know and I'm me

Spat of joy
The earth's grim dimple

Reader I'm ashamed of everything
Feel free to leave

That's right pick up your clutch-bag face
and just go

No wait
don't go

We're having fun aren't we

The trees rise up burn down
The trees rise up and burn down

Spat of joy
The earth's grim dimple

Fee fi fo and no fum

The trap of the world is spun

Or perhaps your take-home ought to come in pieces; parts which you'd assemble at your leisure on arrival chez vous. Or even while you're still on the bus as you travel there, shaking the bag's contents out onto the empty seat beside you, and then sifting through the pieces, so that they begin to marry themselves in your imagination before you muster them physically later on, clicking their male and female connectors together, to create your plaything. I can see you so vividly on that bus, it must surely be real!

Contingency

If you dig a hole and get in it

                    what then

        If you   say   flick a tree and holler

                        well then what

            If you reverse into an attitude

of dotty surrender   all flags flying   the sky as blue

        as an unblown whistle   the children dancing
                what's next for pity's sake

If you ride a horse sideways   the crisp mist coming down all over
        the broom broom

                        The cha   cha

Do you like horses
                    What they say

If you come screaming over the hillocks   the dust and the dust
        A plume in your bonnet

        A cha cha

                        The sheer amount of a horse

You know what side your bread's buttered

                    – both sides

I would be the fabricator of the constituent parts; you, the maker of the finished token. I'd be in a similar position as the manufacturer of paint, who combines pigment with cold-pressed linseed oil, and in some modest way thus contributes, does he not, to the painter's piece of work.

In the wayward place

thin delinquent trees   of that awkward age
loitered
      on a rotten ground

              Fungi convened
                 and conferred

      Inebriated ruins
      drunk on bathtub gin

had fallen into the bramble scrub

         their tiles in disarray
           their underwear exposed shamelessly

      bricks akimbo

     while woodlice fiddled

          down in a befuddled past

birds muttered in shut eggs
the sky was alarming

             it still is

go to the margins

look about

          we are nowhere to be found

Or I will inhabit a grander, more august role, more akin to that of the creative director of a fashion house, or that of an artist presiding over his studio; yes, and you will be my industrious minions working late into the night by moth-bothered candlelight, sewing sequins to a waistcoat, or adding a spatula of Ardent Coral Pink to the scrotum of one of my larger than life self-portrait nudes, abject, lathered in self-pity, on the cusp of his dotage, his twinkle guttering.

When you were dead

you were not alive

so life must have slipped inside you

sidled in
perhaps when your door was left ajar

(no one bothers to lock their doors
in the crimefree provinces of the non)

It must have waited quietly
held its breath in the hallway for a while

before it quickly inveigled
your participant insides room by silly room

That frantic bug surely charmed
your gang of parts before it had them

and then burst out
ripped right out
to strew giggling lights about you

and made you as you are –

entirely discernibubble

See how life makes
such dimpled
tripping clowns of the previously stiff

It waits sometimes in badly lit streets
to suddenly

step out and rob the passive dead
of their crisp straightforwardness

it steals that trustworthy oblivion they've kept
folded in their pockets since forever

and existence now weeps its visions of trees

of streets
of elephants

and of other ones of us
legged
upright
afraid

I can hear you now, making tentative suggestions, when I arrive hungover in the morning and hang my dinted bowler on the hatstand, some tentative suggestions as to a detail of a particular garment or painting or piece of sculpture. Can I trust you tho, to thus collaborate, not knowing who you are?

Puppetry

Now I've seen everything

        toerags have taken the citadel

                shampoo patricians with hidden frills therein

The Blapetty Gardens dug up piecemeal tot by tot

            the town dismantled
            brick by block

       dead d-buried in d-holes

      pinky porcelain

         crocodile treasure

naked throwaways
     all sorts

            (Shall we take a walk in the old town   you and I)

(Shall we pause by the fountains with the knocked off concrete monsters)

The water
    The cracking water wetted

trees b-leafed

       My lady honed to a pin pin pin

Our hands (excited by their quota of ghost)

play under our supervision

The good ol' attendant day

saucisson

the mise en scène

the laws of physics

luncheon

peripheral happenstance

My m-m-m-m-mouth

Your b-b-b-b-mouth

No, I cannot! For I'm certain you'll help yourselves to these fragile remnants, still tender and still raw, (still hot for heaven's sake!), and then use those remnants to do with what you will, making ridiculous alterations and then employing them to adorn some portion of your abode, until you quickly tire of them. I picture you now as you trample through my ruins, small coach parties of you, helping yourselves to souvenirs; at first just those that lie willy-nilly on the floor, but after a short while you're jiggling them free of their niches; don't think I don't see you!

The Trees

a small clique of poplars

               formed a cheery copse down in the long field

they didn't acknowledge us

                    when we trudged past in our outdoor wear

         and seemed to be having a great and innocent time of it

             as they joshed and laughed amongst

                  themselves
                       in patterns arboreal

we may call it laughter

         we may do as we choose

               rooted inextricably as we are
                    to the bitty ground of our domain

indeed if we please

             we might
                 lean right over into theirs

take a long broad
            swing

       and chop them

            taking care they don't come down thisaway

No kind of cow

might mix concrete
because every kind

of shovel

will slip again
and again from between

the cloven toes of their forehooves

No cow

at the end of the long day

as the subtle dusk pulls in

will lean on a shovel

a rollup stuck to
the bottom lip like

an inch of smouldering straw

The cows they did not mix

the concrete sand and gravel

that made their concrete floor

My God, don't think I don't hear the high-pitched, guilty, knick, knick, knicking of the hammers chipping away at what roots my stuff to the ground! Help yourselves you bastards, I am done with all of it!

Quids in

I miss
my pot of gold

(it doesn't jingle because it's a oner)

how I would count
its bounty

its single and delicious coin
that I must pay to quieten

As my old friend Ronnie Corbett would have certainly attested, were he still with us, I am not one to drop names, but I am going to mention here, in an expedient change of subject, that I have met Marcie, though admittedly only once and in a dream. She came into the dry cleaners/ferry terminal/delicatessen where I was operating the steam press in the production of farfalle for the captain's table, and as she stepped through the sliding doors, I broke into a broad smile of recognition, thinking, just for a moment, that we must know one another; her face, her figure, and the way she walked across the room being so familiar to me. Instead of looking away blankly, as one might expect, she returned the smile, albeit fleetingly.

We listened to the cows

to the lolling cows

We mean we listened

to the cows

and all their chunky tongues of breath
on the wrong side of the hedge –

the cow side

A beast is a scattered thing
and all of us have witnessed

the beefs
who doff their heads

who birth their own cuts

who give their splash to the pail

She was, I'm sure, communicating to me that she understood why I had reacted that way on seeing her. I believe she must have known all along that it was me who had made her, just as I had myself.

I adore

the cushty smell my pillow has

It has imbibed my essence
and plays it back to me

on a soft loop

My beguiling
sexy pillow

in its white smock like a saint
with an ancient

baby shame tucked inside like Rome

I am all over the place

I am talky wreckage

I am crumbs at a picnic

I am important ruins

Visit me
Dig me up

Hold me a while to your soft cheek

Now bury me again

I miss

la golden coin

sopped
as they are with light

completely glint

and unspent

tossed
coming up head

tossed
coming up tail

I am not a bad bird

Marcie says

the smallish rain collapses beyond
the leaded you-know-whats

dense quiet of a surrey detached

flowerbeds
english brick

the rain she makes a rumptious dirt of nature

makes room for me

isn't life thick with its impossible girth
and its stupid loll

the candy body broken-in

whispered fucked thunked

look at me
with my

sex in its
knickers like riverdance

now look at me driving my magickey snatch
like a kiss

down a lane
the hedgerows stuffed with piping birds

god help me
I don't care what anyone thinks times two

and look at me still –

my simple knickers

my sauce-pot good-bad scent
scent so funny and hungry and clever as a baby smile

insisting on its own business

its slowly push
its slowly pull

my 1930s scent
stronger then and true

I don't want to say how randy tweed is

in third gear
and Godalming and Haslemere

my own knickers drive me nutty

Marcie says

Graham asked me, *Do ladies like them, to look at I mean?*

and I smiled. *Even Barbara*, I said.

Bless her, said Graham.

If ladies hadn't liked them, I continued,
then evolution would have altered their design

increment by increment till ladies did.

But they look nothing like the other things which ladies like, ventured Graham,
such as jewellery and chocolates and poems.

Well does a cunt look like a Bentley? says I.

It does a bit, said Graham.

How like a man the world is, going round and round and round and round.

Marcie says

Mine and Graham's private parts,
they have more in common with each other

than they do with us.

They'd be so happy together down in the
woods, throwing pinecones, sniffing the wildflowers,

hiding behind the big trees, jumping out and laughing,
playing tag,

scenting the summer air with cute effervescence.

Then out in the big field
that leans down toward the brook

they'd picnic on cucumber sandwiches washed down
with ginger beer.

I can see them now as they lie back and watch
the drifting clouds without a thought in their minds
because they have no minds to speak of.

Hand in hand down by the lake they'd walk
wordlessly, smoking French cigarettes,

or sucking the boiled sweets
they sometimes share, and stiffening a little in the warm breeze.

There's nothing but grit and sunshine
and that delicious hopelessness that makes a privy p to smile.

Marcie says

The Men. How they crave
to board us,

how they long to climb on deck,
and look down

from the crow's nest
at our tits and faces.

Look ahead, Graham!
For god's sake, mind the sandbanks!

Our husbands go to work on land
to get away from just how nice it is

afloat. And all day long they
manufacture spunk in muffled balls

so that they might, on coming home,
ballast us with it

to keep us on an even keel
and floating this way up.

Marcie says

To be concealed is my privilege
To be withheld

Frrrrrgive me then
for the stupid sounds I make

so I might throw you off my scent

so I might
hide from you or something.

So I might cover my tracks before

I've even made them

My approaching tracks
inchoate hollows which await my tread

Your ravenous taste –
it gone and gone

Pull me under
I miss you – as though I ever knew you or something

Are our secrets so well disguised, that in showing them, we hide them further? Is to reveal only to hide; to unearth, to bury; is to come clean, only to come dirty?

Bluebottle Modus Operandi

firstly tempt the suspect truth out
by means of a half-truth

hung like streaky before its hole

let it show its musty face
let it blink and cry a while

pale and soz

let it glimpse the tattletale prints all over the nibbles

as you bend your fingers to examine your thingummies

nails

then jot its recitation

have it lean upon the winkled fruits de mer

let it linger on a prized glass-eye

the periwinkle trick of a shooting star
the lumpy seas
spat pumpkin

all its pretty diversions

A trickled copper ruminates thereupon

We love you lofficer

The entire enchilada
a cypher braced against its own crack

And excuse me, but to whom does that blue and green striped tail belong, the one which protrudes from behind the armoire, and flicks in such a manner that it seems to crossly beckon us?

Cadavre Exquis

      I say
what lenses we have made
out of the air though

spectacles through which we appraise

the shuffled stuff of one another

look at me

how I hold a page

no but

      closer

      so as to be
on this side
of the apparatus

find I am a cave

filled with the treasure someone who loved me hid

a million years ago

help me get at it

Turkey Shoot

I was born

      into

            a

      ladybird building   with slots throughout

and I was slid in 'em   (Still am)

In them slim slots

      Filed
      away
      like
      bees is

Stop it

stop it I have nothing to say

Stop it

      stop it I have nothing to say

except that the future has come and taken everything

I am dispersèd

                                        dissolvèd

Now you see me

                                             Now you see me

                How easy it is to be hunted when you are a   plethora

Birds hammer   Now you see me

All your life is out

a heaving rocken whale
bent on nothing that it knows

whose furrowed back lifts up
and through the roads

and bends and cracks the asphalt
and rises through the fields

the toppled crops
that tumble down its flanks

In the woods trees are
lifted Whoa! and root-first

come down again to totter in their holes

and rabbits bolt
and fray-bugs creak

and under
goes the whale once more to ground

If there was a plan, it was perhaps that he might hide so extravagantly in plain view, and in such an array of preposterous costumes, that he would inevitably be found and taken off, and disciplined and then forgiven. It is the case, it is indeed the closed case, that every person in the line-up is this same assorted character, each as guilty as the next. They all did it, this row of miserable charlatans who in turn must receive her or his justice. One by one they stand head-bowed in the box to hear the beak pronounce the just punishments that will be meted out.

Henry

Look at my mouth

and how she intones a sky

at how she has dirted my corpse
is dirting yours now

and your topsy face

I pulled my la-di-da down by its turvy-string

and then in the throne room
I huggled it headlong

splashed it all over

toe to top

Speak my pie-hole's dollied box then butternuts

Here
have a word –

bite

No wait
have two –

bite me

I see them all, before my eyes, gathered afterwards outside the Old Bailey, having received insubstantial fines and suspended sentences. Look how relieved they are to find themselves purged of their wrongdoings, the slate, for now at least, wiped clean but for a pale smear of chalk, a cheeky streak of ghost. They hug and cry, they dab each other's eyes with their brightly coloured hankies, step carelessly upon each other's long-toed shoes,

A Poisonous Midnight

Mother

     breakneck

     in her open-toed aubusson onesie
     and her fish-skin cloak

is harvesting the figs

the terrace lit
by a steady clatter of rock-hard lamp-given photons

     each is the size
     a sucked on gob-stopper is
     when it's gone

while her too-too elaborate fledermaus
     particularised

     small fur

     minuscule teeth
     one two three and so on

     click click click

     frightened of its life
     and its finger wings

hides in the skirts of the midnight calla lily

making it up

hidden in a lily
skirt lilyskin

     tuck away that bat

       what we are

before, at magic hour, they all go their separate ways, waving those handkerchiefs in excessive au revoir; a troop of immoderate luvvies, each heading to their home.

Hôtel des Champignons

I don't know how it was done,
and neither of us dared go down

to ask at the reception desk,
so fearful were we of discovering

we'd gone mad, and were imagining
what we'd witnessed,

but the motifs on the wallpaper
in our room played the disconcerting

trick of abandoning their locations,
to meander

about the surface of the walls.
They crept as slowly as an hour hand

creeps across its face,
but creep they did.

So that an image
of a French hussar

(one of a few,
as each shifting design

was, as you would expect,
oftentimes repeated),

a mounted French hussar, situated
just above your bedside table

when you first noticed these
unrestrained wanderings,

and drew them to my attention,
had, by the date of our departure

a further three days later,
reached a spot above the wardrobe.

(One could see it clearly,
if one stood on the bed.)

And an inch wide image of a bucolic
lake, once sited by the bathroom

light switch, and which
you had photographed

so we could later verify its
movements, was located furtively

positioned behind the radiator
by the hour we were required

to check out on the Tuesday.
The lake had taken, what's more,

a flamboyantly circumlocutious
path to get to its end point,

as though it meant to insist
that it wasn't following any sort

of preordained itinerary.
We examined the wallpaper closely

as you might imagine, but the more
we touched its surface, the closer

we looked, the more it appeared
like any other wallpaper,

with discernible divisions between
individual sheets,

and even one or two slightly up-bent
corners, just a tiny fraction of an inch

of unstuck paper, as if the glue
had missed those spots.

And then as soon as we stood
further back, the peripatetic designs

began almost imperceptibly
to drift, not as if on a television

or computer screen, but in some
faintly rippling amniotic pool.

Something else we noticed –
When we left to take a promenade

in the Jardin de Luxembourg,
or went out for a meal

in a place we know
in the Marché aux Puces,

then, on our return, we found the images
had remained quite firmly rooted

to the points they had occupied
when we'd left,

however long the duration of our absence,
and seemed only to perform

their peregrinations when we were
present to witness them so doing.

It seemed perhaps an energy saving
device had registered

our departure, and then, having
subsequently detected our return,

switched itself back on, to set
the universe ticking once more.

The other entertainment, if you could
call it that, pertained to the coffee

brought to our room: It stirred itself.
The spoon travelling of its own volition

for a number of revolutions,
and not in a cheap, mechanical fashion,

not like some piece of stiff Victorian
clockwork trickery, or with

the cold falsity of a movie special effect,
but with a ghostly elegance.

How hard it must have been
so well to fake a monkey's grace,

and all of this for an extraordinarily
reasonable €870.00 tout compris.

I'd have liked to have given the hotel
a full five stars,

but as we sat on the train
at Montparnasse,

and I looked out the window
at the adjacent carriage

on the next platform,
I had the distinct sensation

we were moving,
when we most certainly were not.

What fair dumpling

Crocodeelio

What fair dumpling stood across
some precipice of gloom

crock shot
doddered

      You tell me crocodeelio

      You tell me

What lost untethered home of ice slid south
on a sliver of melt

With each inch of slip diminished
Helpless past the bay windows of

      lugged its aura of chill

glid in misery

nipper-followed

dog-licked

Enlighten me crocodeelio
      Fill me in

What preposterous dukedom attired in fanfare
What joy

what circumstance
what ruction

what disarray
what semblances

what brought us here

Button me up crocodeelio

      fold me in

Windows all wound down by thaw
The see-through ceiling drips upon its splashy floor

weeps upon
the par-sucked sweets of furniture

How slow the vanishing home she go

Don't be sad crocodeelio
Everything comes this way

I don't know

if you're familiar

with the kind of box which

every time you flick its switch
to on

reaches out a little hand
to flick the switch off again

My parents, Brian and Monica, and my niece Marina died during the three years I've spent writing this book, as did my friend, the poet, Roddy Lumsden. I want to dedicate it to their memory.

Bacon and Egg

What is bacon
for

if not
for feeling sorry for

Sad bacon
lost her pig

What is egg for
Same

Dismal egg
lost his hen

What more
is there to say

Only this –
Nothing

A winter mist rose off the Hackney Marshes pitches, and the old sun hung still a while longer, before it moved on.